I wonder and Say!

My questions, my answers, and your answers about to:

The questions that come whenever that your thoughts they wonder why those things seem normal, but that are hoped as unlikely in the culture that there is been inculcated in modern life.

Antonio

Hope that all that can give the most natural answers to all the questions that real life proposes.

Summary

3

I am a nerd

But I'm not worth anything, I give birth to plants that are endangered, the gift but no one wants, I write books but I can not sell anyone, I'm just a nerd.

Do you work? I can't do it anymore, I'm almost fifty years old and I still move to see a seedling or a flower open and give birth to such beauty. I know I'm not worth anything. My wife gets angry sometimes with me and almost, not to say always, she's right. But what life is mine I do not know.

I regret so much that this world does not matter to anyone, there are people who for money would cut the legs to his mother, let alone the plants what do you care to saw them, whether they are in extinction or not, it cries my heart In knowing that, even here in

Italy, there have been plants in the critical area of extinction like Abies Nebrodensis that there were only thirty specimens in the Madonie in Sicily, escaped from the blades of chainsaws because they were down a cliff, I have nineteen seedlings because my sister bought a house where there was a plant of Nebrodensis and the seeds fallen to the ground are born and so I took these tiny seedlings and I cured them and now they are beautiful, but not yet large to be planted on the ground.

I say

Why, I say why it must exist so much hatred in the human being to make war to their own fellows even of their own nation, as long as they are different, of their own religion, or because they are different as minorities of another culture, then for this there must be justification for him to war and kill them, just because they are a minority of people that think different from you. I say why it must be like this.

I say why these violent people are not marginalized by society but they find such a broad consensus especially when they have power with weapons, whoever goes behind it more than for a political or religious thought but for the fear of being killed in turn.

What a bad thing to kill people but not only with wars but also states that use the death penalty as an extreme punishment against an individual now in prison and helpless, never kill but not only people but also wild animals and , although it seems a little odd, I also say the trees are still beings living and so do not take away their lives until they have lived their own, because even a tree has the right to die when it is old, and not to saw it as a young man only good to make us wood, that can be done also by the branches of an old tree and from its trunk you can do timber, much more precious than firewood.

I, however, say: never shoot against any man, or animal that is, because it comes one day that you regret what you do, and even if you do not go to jail you will always remain in your heart the mistake that you did.

I had life

I had a wife, and now I have no more.

I had kids, and now I don't have them anymore.

I had a house, and now I have no more.

I had a garden, and now I have no more.

I had a dog, and now I have no more.

I had relatives, and now I have no more.

I had so many friends, and now I have no more.

I had a religion, and now I have no more.

I had a good furniture, and now I have no more.

I had cattle, and now I have no more.

I had chickens and hens, and now I don't have them.

I had rabbits, and now I don't have them.

I had ducks, and now I have no more.

I had chicks, and now I don't have them.

I had geese, and now I have no more.

I had a car, and now I have no more.

I had agricultural machines, and now I don't have any more.

I had woods, and now I have no more.

I had a lake with fish, and now I have no more.

I had so much ground, and now I have no more.

I had so many workers, now I have no more.

I had servants at the table, and now I have no more.

I had cooks, and now I don't have them.

The war came

I had my life, and now I have no more.

Work all four hours

Working all four hours with the usual salary may seem absurd, yes, we'll lose some purchasing power, but you also have to think that we will have the doubling of paid taxes, so you could decrease a little to make more purchasing power to people's salaries.

By doing so, we will remove the hunger in the middle of the world population and the wealth would be a little more distributed, instead of having workers who work so much the eight hours, as there are now, and do not enjoy anything of life and instead have so many people who do not have work and they suffer, so, hunger.

And then, how nice would it be for a person to have half day free? I think more than anything else to those people who do heavy work, very tiring, who work all the life eight hours and when they come to retire they are already finished for the work they have done for life, without enjoying anything of the beauties of our planet and rest everyday half day. The times are ripe now, to realize all that can be done to work all half day, because with the unemployment that is there today, with all the refugees who arrive in Italy, can very well fill the emptiness of the other four hours of the missing work. Certainly decrease the work to four hours you can not do so "at closed eyes", you have to put yourself at a table and make two accounts, but I have the hope that working the four hours only can really do, while maintaining the usual salary. And enjoy a little more life.

To enjoy one's life

I do not know why sometimes the desire to die is so strong, perhaps because I regret for my mother who had a slight stroke and now she walks badly, and to me to see her suffer so it makes me feel so bad.

And then I'm hurt too because I see the total destruction of all the forests of this planet, to get back from the Amazon and so with all the others, all this to run behind the money, waste printed that from a value to everything forgetting that a forest more value when standing, which instead saw dead lying on the ground.

And then I think another thing, that if everyone in this world worked eight hours the destruction of this planet would be total, because we all would like their own new car or used it, we all would like a beautiful house with beautiful furniture, etc. etc. So we must say goodbye to the forests, to the breathing air, because they will be full of carbonate anhydrous.

Instead you have to put yourself in the head to work all less than the current eight hours but work half, work four hours but with this work all, thus avoiding a super consumerism but a minimum consumption that is sustainable from this planet, where we all have the right to live there, and by working four hours we will have twice as many people occupied and so we will have taken away the hunger in the middle of the planet, and we will have half of consumerism, and we could live all better with the money we will have with the usual salary and thus avoid the destruction of the planet as if all we work eight hours around the world.

And enjoy more life that is so short.

The flowers

A flower, how beautiful a flower will be? There are all forms. The first thing you do, when you collect a flower, you bring it to the nose to taste the scent, you put to observe the shape it has. Yes, because every flower, even if of the usual plant, has a different size from each other. Then observe the color, the various shades along the petals, which can be of various shapes, like the irises to the artichokes, the beautiful primroses and the fragrant violets that are among the first flowers that appear in spring. A flower that when it is in the girdle gives birth to a delicious fruit that, after some time, will be ready to eat. It is good and delicious as a cherry.

A flower, that when gifts, brings joy to the hearts of others and each flower expresses a feeling from the chrysanthemums and carnations, to the good wishes roses that each color expresses a feeling, from red to yellow change the words, change the thought.

The flowers, that certain are good to eat, fried or in salad or to make the "pinzimonio" like the artichoke, or put salt as you do with the capers, in short the flowers with their fruits always appear in the tables to eat, or to beautify them or to eat them. And their seeds give birth to a new plant, and the cycle repeats itself as a leader. There are also very flowers that can poison only keeping them in hand such as the Aconitum Napellus, and in the autumn appears the poisonous Colchicum, present in our areas, which makes the very poisonous seeds in spring. The seeds of the Colchicum were used to create the colchicine, an alkaloid isolated from the seeds of the autumn Colchicum that is associated with the polyploidy which is related to sterility for the difficulty of pairing of chromosomes during meiosis, i.e. from a mother cell are formed four daughters cells, with all the reduced chromosomes of number and all different each other cell of the four. In a nutshell it is a cellular and chromosomal modification together.

The Psychiatric Center

Today I want to talk about the psychiatric center where I'm in care.

My doctor is a little old but he is very good at giving the medicine, he knows exactly the effect of drugs and the dosage just to make you feel good enough, perhaps the experience of so many years in psychiatry has made him so well.

However, even the other psychiatrists are good, I have had so many psychiatrists in my twenty years of illness, but I must say that Dr. Luigi, Dr. Sordi and Dr. Francesca, who is now no longer at the psychiatric center, were among the best in my opinion. Anyway with Dr. Luigi, who I have as a psychiatrist now, I find myself well also because He takes care of me very well.

Very kind are also the nurses who bring to the mentally patient a great respect, and do little to bring the medicine to all the mentally people scattered in Casentino. Thanks also to the nurses of the mentally patients.

I must say that even those who answer the phone, the two secretaries are very kind and patients with all the sick who call the center, especially those like me who phone every day even more than once a day, a thank you also to them, and I hope them to be always kind with all the sicks, because when a patient calls, it means that he doesn't feel so good.

Thank you Jesus

Dear Jesus, I know that with this disease that you gave me (depressive maniac) You changed my life, before the disease I was another person; cheap; stingy; I was paying attention to all the money I spent; I did not trust other people; I did not love anyone outside the money; I was always haggling with other people for the price of the stuff I bought; I was always alone; I had no friends points; I was not talking to anyone outside of my family; I didn't even trust my sister, who are in society together in carpentry. I went hunting for birds, I killed them without a reason, yes, then I ate them but from eating I had it already, do not wax need those poor birds. I regretted it so much that I had done it dying so foolishly, just for such a macabre game.

You, Jesus, changed my life with my illness. Today, on the hunt, I do not go anymore and money I do not care anymore, I am no longer stingy and cheap but I love the good of people and nature.

You, Jesus, taught me to love because I did not like anyone outside the money. He taught me that love is worth more than any money that one can have. Today of money I have no more, but I have a family of my own, my wife and my two girls, thanks to you, Jesus, who changed my life, me to love all that you can love. Life of all living being

Thank you Jesus

My mood

Today I don't feel so well, I'm down in the mood. Yes, because it is so: one day you're a little better and then there may be days that you feel more down in the mood, so without a reason.

The mood swings like my thoughts, up and down so for life, and you are not so good. One day you seem to touch the sky with one finger, and another day you want to die. I attempted suicide three times, ingesting psychotropic drugs in so much quantity that they made me gastric lavender for all three times. And believe me sevi I say that you are not so well; they shove a tube from your nose and from there they extract all the stuff you have in your stomach and it's not a nice pleasure to do this, but unfortunately when your head doesn't go, you end up like that.

But unfortunately, pleasure or not pleasure is my disease and I can not do anything outside that cure me with psychotropic drugs. Life, what a funny thing, you never know what happens, when I arrived in the 93 this disease, I thought I was ruined for the whole future life, and instead I got married in the ninety, the year after I had a beautiful girl, named Chiara, and the year after that we still had another girl named Barbara. In short, it has changed my life totally, for the better, and I am very happy that my life has changed so even if the disease has remained, but I am glad it is so that it has set up a family. Today those girls are two beautiful smart girls, brave and I'm very happy.

The Mountain

Today, my wife and I, we were to make a turn in the mountains to see if they wax the paonazze kisses, this is not the scientific name but in our dialect they are called so. We have not found any tips because it is still too early, now we are in May and generally do the month of June because it is hotter.

However we did a nice turn, both on foot and by car, I really needed to go to the mountains, see the beech with the leaves still green clear because recently opened, it is something fabulous to see the mountains covered with trees, I regret only one thing that the trees are only of the usual species so for big extensions without seeing other trees that we could also stay in that climate so cold, alright, better so that nothing. Here in Casentino is full of trees, they are in our mountains that are very beautiful, and it is nice to make us some summer walks when down here, in the valley, it is very hot. It is nice to go to the mountains even when it rains, in September, when the porcini mushrooms are born, feel the water that even if you have the raincoat slips you from all parts and returns home all soft and with few mushrooms.

I had so much fun going to look for the mushrooms when I had the dog named Mina, which I had taught him to find the mushrooms, but only those porcini, the best mushrooms that there can be especially the porcini mushrooms that make the chestnuts very fragrant both to eat fried what a nuisance, I had so much fun with that dog, that when I came the disease, the acute psychosis, I believed that my dog was an angel of God, to help me against the devil I saw in other people. I was very fond of this dog and when she died I did not wish to see why I would have been terrible and so I gave my father the task of burying it.

Today I have another dog named Lola that we took to the kennel, where they put the abandoned dogs, the dog is deaf, blind from an eye and older, but we loved it immediately so much and always comes behind me when I go around in the car and even when I go to make a walk to streets that there are no cars and I can, in this way, I can leave her without a leash, free to run as much as she wants and we have a lot of fun, both her and me.

The war and the pursuit of peace

I would like the world to end wars and all people are well and if they are ill, of any illness, they are treated all indiscriminately by religion or state that they are, I ask too much to you, Jesus, who has forgiven all even while they crucified you, and you said several times to love each other and to give the other cheek if one strikes you. I think that you, Jesus, have taught us a lot but man is hard to understand that peace is the most beautiful thing in the world and hopefully together, me and you, Jesus, that one day the man understands it and stops every conflict.

I do not know, I am crazy that loves all people and I wish health at all, and I also love all the living beings of the planet that you, God, created, and man exploits indiscriminately, whether right or not, all that is to be consumed for your own well-being does not guardand or if in the long term it leads to the extinction of the existing animal or plant species on the planet.

I do not know, dear Jesus, but as long as there will be money and power over other people in the world, perhaps that peace which I have invoked and requested from you will not exist and the wars will still exist. Hopefully the mighty of the earth begin a understanding that the destruction that carries a war and the evil star of the stricken population, lead to think that it is much better peace than the war.

The forest that speaks

I do not know if you ever happened to find yourself in a forest in the mountains, in the morning, just before dawn, and feel the awakening of all the birds that harmonize all the air in a fabulous song to listen to, is a wonderful thing. It happened to me one morning that my mother and I went to look for the mushrooms, because I was wrong to put the alarm clock and set an hour before the due, and so my mom and I left early, finding ourself in the mountains that was still dark and when it began the awakening of the birds, filling the woods with a sweet harmony, and was a beautiful song to listen to. It only happened to me that time, there, but after so many years I still remember it with so much pleasure.

The forest is a place I am very fond of it and I regret so much when I see it burn, both live and on television, I do not know how you can fire a thing so wonderful and full of life, I do not know.

I regret even when they give fire to make room, to graze the cattle, as it happens on other continents too. I have been to Madagascar and I have to say one thing: that from the plane it was an effect to see the rivers in full, of red color as is the land we crossed, it looked like it was blood, of the Earth wounded by the almost total deforestation, and it is bad to see the land without trees for large extensions, and to see it wounded by red landslides of the ground, it makes a strange but ugly effect.

Dear Jesus help me

You, Jesus, do not know if it is only in my sick mind, that you speak to me, or really exists in the minds of all men. I, dear Jesus, I invoke your help, I must ask you for a great thing: to make the man understand that he cannot go on like this, with nature, to prey on everything that interests him, or destroy the stuff of creation because he does not need it and does not care for him.

Dear Jesus, give me a hand to make it clear that we cannot continue to make wars in the name of peace, when we kill innocent or guilty people, they are always human lives and we try to change attitude with them, talking about love and forgiveness, perhaps you can get the usual result without the death of innocent.

You Jesus, you must help me to understand this to all the rulers of the world, to all those who have power to change things, because the earth is of all, good or bad, which may seem, whether they are animals or plants or human persons. Let's try to bring peace, with words, in the world and not with bombers or missiles and bombs so called: clever. That of intelligence, there is a little otherwise they would not be thrown. I ask all the heads of state to resolve the divergences, with other people, using the words, those, yes, which are weapons of peace. Please, Jesus, help me to change the world that so, to me, does not like.

My illness and my proposal

Mentally patients are seen, from other healthy people, with distrust, as if all mentally patients are as dangerous as we paint television, especially maniacs, as I am: depressive maniac.

The television, that to throw mud on people even sick does not think twice. And so, people, they look at you with distrust as you have leprosy and do not evaluate people for what they are really, good or bad they are. Yes, I am manic depressive and I have had luck in finding a woman, very good, who is with me, despite my illness, but she knows that I am not bad, indeed from the times he tells me that I am a jerk because maybe seen from his eyes are good, however I feel like all other people because I care with psychotropic drugs. My only flaw is with the mood: that is not too good and sometimes I feel down and I am very sad, this happens to me, especially when I see people getting hurt, this depresses me a lot, for this I often write about people who are sick and are in misery or they are victims of wars, this regret me a lot and make me feel bad. I was in Africa, in Madagascar, and there I saw in the face the real misery, which is much worse than how they show up on television: in the capital there were sewers at open sky and people had a great misery. For this I say: we work less still hours around the world but we give the possibility to people to work all and remove from the misery half world population. And then as I said other times: work less and enjoy more life.

Also because if everyone in the world we work eight hours the destruction of planet earth would be total, already now we are at the limit that the planet can endure with the increase of greenhouse gases. So my proposal is to work less than four hours but work all.

The Terrestrial Paradise

I already believe that I am in the terrestrial paradise. It is so beautiful nature with its diversity of plants, animals, birds, fish, which makes me feel already to live in the terrestrial paradise. And the sea will be beautiful with its sunny beaches, and under the sea, with its corals and its fish, it is a marvel.

I do not know why man has closed in factories, offices, working eight hours, instead of enjoying this paradise, instead of postponing this desire to live well only when The pension will arrive, not calculating that when we get to the pension we are already finished and our dreams are no longer done. We often work all the life enjoying only that month of vacation, as if it were an award due, and not a lifestyle.

I do not know maybe I am mistaken in thinking of being in God's creation in his terrestrial paradise, where all men should enjoy it not one month a year but the goal of the year, and so enjoy life on this planet and not do a cross to work all day.

Life is so beautiful, enjoy as long as we are in the world, we change the laws that regulate the work, so much a super production does not serve anyone outside of those who command us that they make a good life, and the workers make it ugly.

Mental illness

My illness that the morning does not forgive me to get sick with the depression that does not leave me free a minute with its sadness and sometimes with the desire to die, yet I take the medicine every day and as prescribed by the doctor.

From the times I hear in my head Jesus, I do not know whether they are auditory hallucinations or pseudo hallucinations however of these hallucinations I am not afraid because I always talk about things to do or write always with goodness and love.

Mental illnesses are tremendous you never get to feel good, you can feel good for a few days but never solve the problem because the mood changes every day and so you always go up and down your whole life.

Let us hope that God will help me in life never to lose control of the situation. The only good thing is when I talk with Jesus thought that is something that I like because it always speaks of beautiful things.

But in life as a young man I would never have expected to become a crazy day and so I care for the madness but reluctantly because it is not a good thing to tell, even if I do not ashamed at all.

Criticism of my books

My wife told me that I write all the crap, it hurt me a lot, because what I write I write it with my heart and are my feelings more heartfelt and dearer. It made me doubt whether I do well to write them or not, I put all my heart to express my dearest feelings and such affirmation dictated by a loved family person throws you down a little. I have been sick for a few days then the urge to express myself is shooting me facts now I am writing. Some friends find what I write very interesting while someone else also finds him that I write all the crap. The thing hurts me a little too because to tell me is my dearest friend, I do not know who has reason, I continue to write or my wife and my friend with their statements. Perhaps they do not understand that writing something to everyone can not please, there is enthusiasm for someone in reading my books and someone describes them as they were all crap. However from these statements I have resumed and now start writing again, also because with such writings I want to leave a memory of me to my children and my grandchildren, who remember who was his father when I will not be there anymore, remember so much better that a photo you can now and then the memory desappear, while a book makes you remember better than who was that person and what feelings he had, hindsight you pass on this planet without leaving a memory of anything and away.

The walk in a forest path

I have found a new friend Viola, with her we go for long walks in the mountains and here closer where there are roads that do not pass cars, it is because with us we always carry our two dogs that make us company in our walks.

This walk in the mountain's woods makes me come back to mind when I was younger than I had long walks in the woods in search of mushrooms with my dog Mina who has now been dead for so long. It's great walk in the woods, hear the chirping of the birds that interrupt the air from silence in a sweet harmony that cheers your heart and opens your mind that makes you think of how beautiful nature is in all its aspects. Along the streets on the edge you can see a world of flowers to my beautiful eyes, ranging from primroses, violets, and other flowers of which I do not know the name, to the wonderful orchids, in short a wonderful harmony of colors that disappear with the arrival of the summer.

The mountain that gives us with its woods things that with the eyes we can not even see, as the oxygen very precious for life on our planet, and these immense woods do their job of giving oxygen in a grave silence almost tell us please let us live that we make you live. It is the importance of a forest that lives and makes other living beings live.

The biggest sin

The biggest sin is no longer if a woman betrays you if you do not know how many women should be stoned with all marriages that end because they betray, or if a man kills another man, if not you know how many soldiers should go to jail, or whoever steals or makes armed robberies if you don't know how many corrupt politicians with bribes should go to jail.

Today I return to repeat that the biggest sin is not against people but it is against nature the greatest sin, against the wild animals, against the trees, against the earth to pollute it with anything, from the radioactive waste of nuclear power plants to borina of nylon that if by chance ends up at sea is ingested by some fish, sin is also who throws in the air any toxic substance with the tube of escapement of the cars of which I am also part of, to the power plants that produce electricity that throw in the air anhydrous carbon that causes the greenhouse effect, which I also avail of.

This world is a chain of which we all belong, and we pollute and destroy it with our way of life is a mechanism set in motion from which we are all part for the destruction of our planet Earth this is the real sin bigger, of which day after day without reflecting without even thinking about it, out that those four idiots of ecologists of which I put myself, who remind us every so often that we are destroying the planet, our house, without even realizing it.

This is the biggest sin

Ecology

I am just a passenger on this land spaceship, a passenger as one of the millions of men who inhabit this world, one that does not count anything and has no voice in anything because I am mad, discarded by the healthy society.

The world I dream of is a world that those who command the government have another aspiration instead to make money or reign as a dictator, but to love their people, to love their own land and protect it from those who make it a bad use, as Inquinandola with residues of all kinds.

The land in which we live is the only place in the universe in which man can live, and people must understand that there are hundreds or thousands of animal and plant living beings in the critical area of extinction, after which there are no more, disappeared from the earth.

For this reason a good government should recreate the appropriate environment to try to save as many species as possible from extinction, because it will be a day that we realize that we have made a splurge, run everyone behind the money printed paper and do not open the eyes to see that we are destroying our house.

People, the majority live in cities similar to large hives and do not care anything if it disappears from the world a plant to which insects and animals are connected, or collapsed an ecosystem to make way for a forestry that is only one species of tree, beech-wood, fir-wood, pinewood, chestnut copse, forests of only oaks, it is so destroyed all an ecosystem just because a man returns more comfortable to have only one essence all together because so grouped you do first to work it and earn in less time more money and so they disappeared from our woods plants that today even the imagination does not make them weigh that there had been, like: the largest ash is no longer, the linden is no longer , the yew is no longer, the mulberry and the moor are no longer there, the platinum is no longer, the elm although there was the disease and many died there are varieties that resist the disease, but are not reintroduced and so even they are no longer , the horse chestnut also he is no longer, the maples outside that in the national park outside there are no more, the holly is no longer, I could consulting the books continue yet but that's enough, all this disappearance from our woods depends only on having done the forestry to earn more money, and destroy all the ecosystem connected to these trees, to bushes of plants that in the forestry there are no more, and animals and insects also disappear from that environment no longer having their microhabitat, so wild bees butterflies and other insects of which I do not know the name can also extinguish, and animals like the lynx, and birds like the oriole, the hawks, the buzzards no longer see, instead animals and birds that live from the waste of the man increase as, crows seagulls, starlings and crows etcetera.

For me, the destruction of the land of our country goes to the bottom of having chosen to do forestry.

Never shoot

You never kill a man even if at the moment it may seem like your enemy, because as he teaches us the most recent history those who in the Second World War were our enemies today are the closest allies in economy and as friends, but having tightened the rifles and more, against each other can exist a little grudge and this thing is ugly between allies. For this I have said so many times that it is better not to shoot even if it is an order of your superior because a person is always worth more than an order given by whoever it is. But I say another thing, never kill even wild animals if you do not have the strict need to feed because they also have the right to live as they are free animals and not bred for the purpose of feed. Life is a good too precious to remove it from someone even if it is a condemned to death always respects the life of this person and never kill it, for the simple reason that it is a living being and for more a person.

And you fisherman even if you fish prunes remembers that are even always fish free in the water and if fish not good to eat do your best to put them back in the water alive because even if they are not good for eating they always serve as something because they are still living beings and must be respected.

I say one thing, that your enemy today can be your best friend of tomorrow.

My friend hallucination

Oh Jesus, it is nice to be able to speak, I do not know maybe you are just a pseudo hallucination but I like to have you in my thoughts give me courage in what I write and help me to try to write things that I and you feel useful to write. Criticize a little all the system that man does, from the greatest sins to the relationship that man to with nature and his fellows, thank you Jesus to help me hindsight I would not know how to write all of my thoughts, I would not even know which way I would refarm to write one. I know you're not an hallucination but just a pseudo hallucination, but I'm really excited to have you in my thoughts, always help me try to do my best possible in everything I do both in the book and in life trying not to give boredom to anyone including my family and other people. Thank you Jesus for all that you do for me that I am just a sick man with a bad illness that sometimes makes me feel so bad until I get to try suicide by ingesting handfuls of psychotropic drugs, thank you Jesus for all the help you give me in my life and my family and of all the people that I am close to, I wish everyone a good health that is that most counts in life, a thank you to all my friends who they endure me every day. And a thank you to Jesus who helps me to go on in life day to day, really thank you Jesus.

The air

The air that we breathe the insozziamo with everything and often we forget that we breathe second after second, minute after minute, and yet you have to remember that the air is a precious asset more than any diamond that exists on the face of the earth, and we do not give it weight, we remember it only when they remind us that the carbon dioxide is rising.

The air we breathe we forget that it is free and that is why we do not give it a value even if there is. The trees and algae of the sea give us the oxygen that we breathe, quietly without making noise give us this good so precious, but it will come a day that you have to choose or the wood to work or the air to breathe, if you continue to throw down trees in the forests as we do today in a reckless manner. The air that when we enter a forest to breathe the scents and take some breath of air because it feels so pure and fresh. We never forget that the trees the air will damage us for free as long as we love them and we feel part of them on this planet even if that land belongs to to others the trees belong to everyone and when you see it knock down someone species if big sorry at all.

I hope that my thoughts like you

In writing my thoughts from the times I repeat myself because to write a booklet so it takes me a year and so I forget the thoughts written before you because not every day I feel good to write, this disease I have (manic depressive) does not make me feel good every day, and so from the times spend weeks I do not write and by chance in one day I can write also two of thoughts. Anyway, the only thing that makes me happy is if you like it, from times to my friends someone likes it and to another no, and then not all thoughts are beautiful someone more and some other thought is more ugly, not all I get equal goes based even as I feel psychic mind not every day are the same, I'm sick that I can do if I got sick the best piece of a man's brain, to me happened this to someone else you can get sick of another thing, we are men not machines we try with the meds to stay a little better but the recovery in my case has not arrived, and I am so sorry.

However, the important thing is to go forward in life, if I was born in the middle ages maybe they would burn me alive as it happened to the poor mentally ill who had the mystic delirium and were seen by people as skelter and no as mentally ill.

However, coming back to us fortunately there are medicines that even if you do not heal, allow us to move forward in life.

Holiness Pope Francis

Holiness

I write this letter to make it aware of a powerful remedy for natural health, the Aronia Melanocarpa a good plant that the good God has given us to cure ourselves naturally.

It cure, cancers, diabetes, heart varicose veins, blood circulation by making the veins more elastic, the blood pressure and always taking the medicine prevents the altering sclerosis not allowing to do lumps in the blood treating Alzheimer's and against cell aging by rejuvenating them increases the memory makes slimming diminishing appetite. And so many other things that I don't remember now, anyway I invite you to look in the computer to see what it's good for.

It's just a fruit juice of this plant and nothing more, I take half a glass every morning is a bit hostile and gives the nausea but it does so well that it is better to take it and I hope in the future to stay best. I wish a long life for you holiness and to pass it as much as possible into health, kind regards holiness hoping to have given you a good advice. I embrace you strongly Antonio Piantini.

The Aronia can be purchased on Www.martinavip.com

A star coming from the east

A star coming from the East, an exceptional star, just so came from Poland for the fate of us to meet, and so today is my wife.

I'm so in love with her even though it's been eighteen years since we got married, a simple wedding with twenty-two guests.

The beauty is that to take her to the church, I was own me with the car A UNO that still owns it and still goes even if she is twenty-two years old and I keep a lot of account because it is my father's memory that the new buy in the hundred ninety its first new car, it kept it so much of account and I am so honored that it is touched on me.

In short, returning to my wife when we knew each other she was the most beautiful girl I had ever known, was beautiful, and I fell in love immediately and after seven months we get married. I repeat it I know but it was beautiful with that indescribable face from how beautiful it was and then if one looks at her with eyes to love it is even nicer. I have a good memory of those moments when you met and you get married and even if you have passed many years I am always in love with my wife and I wish her all the good possible.

She is so good she keeps the house clean as a lumen and always carries my daughters where they want them, in short my wife is very talented and I want her huge good.

Change jobs

If you are an arms manufacturer change craft, grow wheat so you can feed people.

If you are an arms manufacturer change craft, put yourself to make bread so you can feed people.

If you are a manufacturer of weapons change craft, think of love among peoples and put yourself to build tractors to ship in the third world so you can help to cultivate the land even in those places.

You worker who manufactures weapons, changes the craft and cultivate the land to feed men and animals.

If you are an arms manufacturer, think about the death that you give to animals or people and change craft and grow rice so you can feed people.

If you are an arms manufacturer change craft and put yourself to manufacture agricultural machine so you can help people to cultivate the land and so they can feed and live.

However if you manufacture weapons you surround yourself with death both of animals and people and it is not a good thing, try to change your production because the machines you have to work can build life to help people or death with weapons, think about it because by you depend the life or the death.

A bag of medicines

My life is tied to a bag of medicine, I try from the times with the opinion of the psychiatrist to take a little less but I am immediately sick, that passion, I will never make it to heal now I have made a reason not to heal anymore. I never wish anyone to have any mental illness is getting very bad though from the times you're a little better you can never say I'm fine because the next day you're hurting again. In my depressive manic illness you're hurt especially in the morning when you get up from bed with a funeral mood, that turn of... the afternoon generally you're a little better but still having a sick brain is always a torture.

Do strange things how to raise 1200 giant sequoias just because they are vulnerable to extinction and other plants because they are in the critical area of extinction, it is crazy, fortunately or found of the people who took it because they love plants all dates free because no one buys them, and then thank them even because the year taken and the weeping. But it's just crazy to do so, that I can do it if when I get an idea I can not help but realize it, I'm just crazy I think back to bring birth to a thousand and two hundred redwoods, but. However, it is the illness of a mentally ill, and there is nothing to do.

The Misery

Misery is ugly, but it is even worse when others make you weigh on it because in that system you humiliate yourself as a person not on equal with others and so you feel marginalized by that society, that those who have a lot of money and power all lick their feet and are friends, and who is in misery has few friends because others are afraid that they are asked for money, but those few friends of those who in misery are, those are true friends in the sense of the word.

I have been in Africa and I have seen in the face the real misery for this I understand well who escapes from those places to look for luck in other states, does not care to make so much money but just be able to live decently because for those who escape from those places is already a luxury.

If you have little money and you have an disabling illness you are in misery even in rich countries because they are few who help you free only because you are their friend, out that the closest relatives others care highly if you are in misery, anyway you see the real friends when you ask them for money to survive not huge figures but little money, the tight needed to live there you can see real friends. The money you all will moves around those and so you will close our eyes to not see what are the true riches like friendship the freedom and riches of the whole world that surrounds us, from nature has everything that man has built in the millennia since his birth.

Protecting the territory

A state that does not protect its territory but is only attentive to economic growth, is a state that is not worth anything because its own well-being is in protecting the land that gives it the fruits to eat and to pollute the earth is tantamount to poisoning himself from drinking and the eating every day and so it's not good, because drinking water and eating that is the primary good of a nation, and a good government must keep this problem in mind by protecting from pollution every terrain is public and private by those who pollute it both with chemical residues and radioactive residues because these substances scattered in a territory are all to be finished in the aquifers poisoning them for kilometers and kilometers and these waters with the artedian wells that irrigate the fields cultivated for both the man and his animals to eat we find them in dishes from all over the world who buy those products.

And so it is not good to run all behind the money and not giving the maximum value to these things that we find them in the mouth all, and every day.

Another maximum value should also be given to the reforestation made without giving value to the diversity of plants that go to reforest by placing more varieties per hectare without making large plots of land with only one species of tree because that means destroy entire ecosystems without having more microhabitats provided instead by a variety of multiple trees planted for each hectare. So planting several different trees will feed you to more animal species whether they are deer up to the smallest butterfly or bird it is.

Jesus what do you want from me

What do you want from me Jesus, I am just a poor fool who cries in his writings of how I see the world and I sue what in my opinion is wrong, simple things but that I think are wrong in my books you find all my thoughts and what is there that It doesn't go to this world.

I said that I think the reforestation with big extensions of only one species of tree so it's not good because it destroys everything that is the microhabitat that exists in every single tree species no longer found in the big extensions of trees of one species, then I said to saw the trees when they lived suit their lives and not by little ones. I said to work all just four hours because if everyone in the world worked eight hours the world would not make it to sustain a super consumerism, so it's best to work all but only work four hours and with these hours to be able to camp the family.

I said to stop sawing the trees because they already do not make it anymore to absorb all the carbon dioxide produced by the consumerism of the man of its power plants and cars and all the motor vehicles to burst and no, and all the heating of the dwellings of man.

I said stop polluting the earth with any harmful substance to the environment because then it ends all under ground and goes to pollute the aquifers and with the artesian wells that are used to irrigate the crops we find it in the dishes we eat and in the water that we drink every day. I said stop polluting the air that we breathe because then it all ends up in the lungs and we find ourselves poisoned without even knowing why it happened.

I said stop making wars that only lead to the death of innocent people and the destruction of homes that to make them to a family takes a life and a second to destroy it.

I have said so many other things that now do not come to mind but these are the most important.

Jesus can you help man to be conscious of the damage he does for himself and for the house in which he lives,

THE WORLD

The Poison Factory

He was a young boy when he saw the ditch near his father's factory, with the water dyed black, it was so because his father had a tannery of the skin, and used the clean water to tanne the skin, and then threw it into the ditch after using it and polluted with all the chemicals used in tannery, without purifying it without even thinking that so poisoned all the water of the river in which the water of the ditch spilled. Time passed and the fish of the river slowly died and were disappearing from that river which was highly polluted.

In the tannery factory many people were working perhaps more than a hundred and so no one had the courage to denounce this pollution for the fear of shutting down the factory and sending all those people home. The time passed and so also the pollution of the river increased and the fish in the river were no longer there. Even the son of the industrialist had grown up and soon took the factory management of his old father, who was retiring.

The son, however, had an ecological conscience, so given the damage that his factory brought to the environment decided even if this cost a lot of money to put a purifier to the dirty waters of the tannery, thus returning in the ditch clean water. This example was also taken by other leather tanners of the valley, so doing all together return to the river clean water and so he could return to life in the river, and they saw back to live the fish and shrimp sign of a clean water. Unfortunately, for groundwater, nothing could be done, causing years and years of superficial pollution that had penetrated down the water.

But it could be said that with goodwill the man could also change a river making it livable after much pollution made by tanneries, bring life back to a river with fish and shrimp, a record for the environment of those places.

The hunting

To shoot those poor critters, what they did wrong to be taken to shoot. I went hunting and if I could make I could give back their live because they did not done nothing wrong, I regretted myself bitterly and every time I hear a shot I pray for the hunter who realizes the mistake he does and he regrets a day like I did and I was sorry so much. I hope long life to all the animals even the most boring ones that do harm to the crops of man or as the bears and wolves that fear the man because he is afraid to be attacked and can be harmed. I now love all the animals and if a hunter reading this writing I opened his heart and stopped hunting I would have gotten a great result and I would be very happy and I would have reached my goal to open the heart to a person.

Hunting or war are the usual thing only that by hunting you do the war against an unarmed enemy, which as defense only has the escape and so it is not fair and even loyal to fight against a unarmed enemy. I hope that this writing reads a hunter and repents for the wrong that he did and can convince other hunters to stop hunting which is a bad thing.

The plant that cure me

I have always said that every tree or bush that gives fruits or leaves always serve for something or for the animals or for the man.

My brother before leaving for Poland to go to my wife's house, he told me to see if I found the plants of Arona Melanocrata, it is a plant that makes fruit in grapes that ripen in black color and from these fruits extracts a liquid that is good for both arteriosclerosis and Alzheimer. This plant grew in the cold areas of North America and was already known by the Indians of America as a medicinal plant for man.

My sister-in-law has bought a bottle of this fruit juice and I started drinking it on the first day not knowing the healing power of this plant I drank half a glass however my wife told me that dosage was too high so the next morning I took a cup of coffee and immediately began to make effect in his medicinal power but the dosage was still too much. The following day I took only half a cup and I have to say that I felt an improvement of my psychic mood, I was amazed that the juice of a plant can make such a strong effect in my psyche and in my relationship with the food that from living to eat until I get to the weight of 155 kilograms, to eat for live that I have now. In addition I also lowered the blood pressure, so when I return to Italy I will feel the doctor if I can stop taking one of the two tablets that I lower the pressure bleeds.

I've always said that plants heal us and now I had the proof on me.

Who are we common people?

Who are we common people, who reminds us after our death and how we are remembered, and by whom we are remembered, are you ever asked? I think many people have done and they have left the fate to lose. I instead want to be remembered when I am dead for my thoughts for what I have done in life for who I have been, for this I write books on what I think and what I did when I was alive to leave it to my relatives and my friends , I want to be remembered for who I am, that I did born a thousand and two hundred giant sequoias and are scattered throughout the Casentino and also elsewhere, which I made a dog that sought only porcini mushrooms, which I did the carpenter who then after I was sorry a lot because I did sawing so many trees around the world , so I write because I will stay alive for everyone who knows me for what I wrote, that I had a psychosis then after the depression because they are manic depressive in short I am what or written and nothing more. These my books I wrote are my life as mentally ill and when I was not yet sick in sum I am so, that I had three gastric lavande that for now I have not sold even a book but I have them all gifted to friends and relatives as I have given all the Sequoias and and other trees all vulnerable to extinction in short I love this world, and I regret one day leave it though as they do all I have to leave it but I'm sorry, but they will remain my writings and that's it. I hope those who light them understand who I was and have a good memory of me.

The unconsciousness of man

The white man thinks with his work to change the world to his own liking, but it will be the world with his climate to change him.

Already the climate will change the man from his way of plundering nature especially the trees, which with their work of consuming carbon dioxide diminish the greenhouse effect of the planet.

But I do not know if the man will understand it in time to stop throwing down trees or it will understand too late to get to the point that the climate is too changed and do not do more in time to return to the back.

The trees the weakest beings on the planet, who with their work to create oxygen year made livable our planet, but already from now they do not make it to consume all the carbon dioxide created by the man who wants to be the master of the world. But the man thinks to do as the master of the world because it will be the world to change him, in his way of behaving in comparison to nature.

The man in his thirst to consume wood throws down trees for both the wood and to make room for his own cattle and does not realize the damage that makes to the nature of the whole Earth globe.

Hopefully it's not nature that brings us the bill.

The Universe for me

Where you are, there is my house.

Where you are, there is my life.

Where you are, there is my family.

Where you are, there is my treasure.

Where you are, there is my wealth.

Where you are, there is my fortune.

Where you are, there is my love.

Where you are, there is my heart.

Where you are, there is my world.

Where you are, there's my bed.

Where you are, there is my peace.

Where you are, there is no war.

Where you are, there is my sun.

Where you are, there is my land.

Where you are, there's my water.

Where you are, there's my fire.

Where you are, there is the hope of a better world.

Where you are, there is my source of life.

Where you are, there is peace for my illness.

Where you are, there is sincerity.

Where you are, there's the interview.

Where you are, there are no lies.

Where you are, there's everything I want from life.

Where you are, there is my church.

Where you are, there are my little girls.

Where you are, there's my roof.

Where are you, Maria there is the whole universe just for me.

My dream

If I do not change anything in the world, for the vision of the world that I have, it means that my passage on this planet has not served anything.

I would like my thoughts to come to the powerful people of the planet and share them at least in part. I know that they are megalomaniacs thoughts but it is my life and if I do not change anything especially in the vision that I have of the environment in which you live, I do not feel realized and mean that I am a nerd, because in life you have to dream something that you want to realize all those people do, and this is my dream.

Does this planet love us because it makes us live and we in the world love it as well?

I do not know if we are worthy of this planet that we from all its most precious goods, the oxygen, the water, the land to be cultivated, its trees from both fruit and beauty, the grain the rice that all of us feed, all the fruits of the garden, animals and fish to eat or not, just for company like the dog the cat the horse and more.

This planet gives us too much of his love that he has for us, and we what we make to this world, immonde, environmental pollution, radioactivity, and all the sozzerie that makes the man poisoning even the aquifers that give us a drink, with abusive landfills even with radioactive waste. We are the worst animals that this planet has. We're going to pay for two bucks, and you kill yourself with soldiers for power over other people. We are not worthy of this planet, which gives us all his love.

AAA Life

A, life, that when you are young you look very long and you have all the desire to do something and you never stop, and when you get to fifty years and throw the sums you realize you have not enjoyed anything of your life spent every day working to do that, one more house or one more piece of land. Having so many things that you can't keep them, I'll tell you that it's not worth it to close for eight hours inside a building to work all how many days enjoying only that month of the year of vacation. That's why I say to work only four hours a day but work all, because in the world we are many and you can not work all eight hours the world would not make it to sustain a super consumerism and the super production by all , for this I repeat working four hours but working all around the world to divide a little the wealth that comes from work, and the rest that advances enjoy the life that we have one, and then to do that work eight hours when with the machines that are there today to work the earth the eating advances to all and the rest of the work to do that, to make more houses than when we have one for family we advance. A life, that when you are fifty years old and you throw the sums you realize you have thrown it all away inside a shed or office that is, until you stand up as it happened to the leg of my sister or to become as crazy as I am. I recommend you young people of the future change the laws concerning the work, and share this wealth of work in four hours a day for all those with the usual salary of eight hours, since there are no more in the world people in misery and those who have so much " The work, "and go treasure of these words that I say, that so much to eat there is for everyone, and enjoy life until you enter this infernal machine that is the work of eight hours a day. And then it is not an impossible thing to work four hours and collect as the current eight hours, because the state will receive twice the contributions and thus will have to halve the taxes, both to the companies and the VAT making so remain high the purchasing power of the salaries. Then it will be a thing to studying for good, but I don't think it's an impossible thing.

My mood today

Today is not going, I want to die, I am a nerd, because I wonder why Jesus gave me a brain crackpot, that of days he wants to do something and there are some days that I have a funeral mood. So it's not good, the best piece of a man I have sick, today just do not make it very bad or Jesus Jesus what patience it takes me, that balls excuse the word.

Life, to those who gave so much and to whom sickness and pain even if this pain is the psychic, and it is very bad, and it is difficult from other people to understand this because one day they see you feel good if I have luck a little more days and then returns the depression, how much is bad this name for the person has on it.

I only have a fortune compared to so many other mentally ill people to have consciousness of my illness and for this I always take the medicines and so I do not need to do the bites of psychotropic drugs but I take them only by mouth several times a day. Who does not have this disease is difficult to understand and for this I write even if I am ill to let others understand my pain that has led me three times to try suicide, ingesting handfuls of psychotropic drugs. But having the brain that doesn't go is really ugly.

When he is born

When a calf is born, it is a joy for the peasant.

When a chick is born, it is a joy for the child.

When a kitten is born, it is a joy because it is young.

When a seed is born, it is a joy because it will give a frutticino.

When a kid is born, it is a joy for the beak.

When a lamb is born, it is a joy because it is beautiful.

When a flower is born, it is beautiful because it brings love.

When a small dog is born, it is a joy for the Mas'r.

When a plant is born, it is a joy because who eats it.

When a tree is born, it is a joy to plant it.

When a turkey is born, it is nice because it is cute.

When a blackberry is born, it is nice because it is good.

When a horse is born, it is nice to mount it.

When the grass is born, it is good for the calf.

When a beautiful child is born, it is a joy because it is the first.

A day so

That boredom stay in the world, this morning I woke up that it was four and a half and I could no longer sleep so I got up trying to make as little confusion as possible and I'm gone to take my half glass of Aronia and then I took the psychotropic drugs and had breakfast with a bit of pizza advanced from yesterday and the milk and coffee. My day started so I watched a bit of television but I get bored right away so I took the computer and I read two pages of what the Aron does well and then I put myself to write on the computer what you are now reading you. At half past ten I have to go to the dietician to do some accounts on my weight that the past week was five pounds and a half and this week instead is 148 pounds, nice progress I did in my diet instead of slimming I'm fattened but I'm not worth anything.

Today I give away all the redwoods less badly that I managed to give her away all hundred giant sequoias I had just lucky to place them all giving. This time I gave them to the daughter of Mauro La Vanna who lives near that place of Reggello where there are a hundred redwoods, the biggest italian Sequoieta so fascinated by these giants of nature she want to plant them in her own soil.

The future in my opinion

As I see the future of man.

First of all will be taught in schools the brotherhood between peoples and respect for foreigners, then always in schools will be taught to love nature in all its forms, from the trees to the smallest insect and animals that are.

There will be a reduction in working hours, from the current eight hours to four hours of work to allow all the work with the usual salary of the current eight hours of work.

There will be an increase in electricity production by mainly wind and photovoltaic plants to allow a saving to be made to use the electricity to heat the houses in winter.

There will be a big awareness of the ecology on our planet until the cutting of the trees ceases especially in the lungs of the earth, such as the Amazon rainforest and all the large forests scattered across the planet.

There will be a restoring of our forests by reinserting trees now disappeared from our woods.

There will be a big drop in carbon dioxide due to the man for the big savings due to the consumption of electricity produced mainly by the wind farms distributed throughout the planet.

The world I would like to

The world that I wish it to be should be full of love for everything, both for nature and among people. I have read the gospel twice and I think it is one of the most beautiful books never written and it would be nice to be put into practice by the man at least in part. Jesus who in his talk taught us so much and the juice of the Gospel is the eleventh commandment what Jesus said himself to love the neighbor as himself, and perhaps is the most imported among all the commandments, I am nothing in this world , but I would add another commandment to love the planet Earth as oneself, because in this world there we live all the nature and the men and the earth that it gives us its fruits and even if it is not cultivated but there are only trees give us the most precious good the oxygen that we breathe and gives life together with water and earth to all. And that is why we must love the planet Earth with all our hearts and punish those who do not want him well polluting whether it is a state or a single person.

And every day to me this world is polluted by both cars and power plants to produce electricity and more, tact is that carbon dioxide is increasing and often with abusive landfills is polluted also the aquifers that then we draw the water both for drinking and to water our crops. And that's not good.

Tomorrow is another day and you will see

Tomorrow is another day, and you will see.

I can no longer see people dying in wars around the world, or the refugees dying because of this emigration with these barges arriving in Italy from North Africa for the hope of finding a better world than they are fleeing because often of wars. Or because I wonder that the world is so, that man has so much hatred for his fellows, I do not know how to find an answer, but I am so sick for all this dying of people.

And then when they come to Europe what they believe to be welcomed with open arms, is no not so, they are often put in these sheds with a barbed fence all together and then returned to their own countries of origin. But if the world is so, I don't want to be part of this world.

But that man is so I do not understand it, in stead of accepting these poor people, and give him a job, a house where to live are treated in stead as beasts, I do not understand. Hopefully it changes the way you see these people, because being in the 2000s and not solving this problem is not right. But if the problem is to give it a job to be able to camp and so keep up, we solve this problem. I have an idea already, as I have already said so many times in my book the problem is solved by halving the hours of work and giving work so to so many people, even our unemployed so they can work, and twice the people will be able to have this precious good that is the job.

In doing so throughout Europe, all these refugees will be able to accept and thus give them a dignity of human beings, and not be treated like beasts. And then where it is written that a man must have to work eight hours to camp, they can not decide the states all together to halve the work to give so work to all with the same salary of the eight hours of work. It would have solved a big problem, so you can solve the problem of the super production that there is already, there would be in stead the double of consumers who will thus buy the products of the super production.

We hope that the man understands that you can span the same working less, but work all around the world.

Please Jesus bring me to heaven

Jesus please take me to the sky, I do not make it to stay down here there are wars there is the destruction of forests the pollution of the whole planet warming the whole Earth with the increase of carbon dioxide, the man does not respect at all his house that is the world he wants to dominate it from all sides this poor world does not want to leave them even an unexplored centimeter where nature can do its course, but man must plunder the whole planet. I'm not well down here, please Jesus bring me to sky. People get angry even for a honking of the car, people are also offended by a word or fact that they do not come back well they also come to kill themselves for a trifle. And then the more serious thing you kill for money, this damned waste printed that turns all the people of the world, this is absurd. I beg you to bring me to sky, where there is your peace and love for all, thank you Jesus for your teachings that bring to rest in my heart, thanks for all this Jesus.

The man down here has lost the meaning of life and how precious it is for every living creature of the whole planet, keeping off it with the tracks of the tanks always ready to shoot cannons.

A thank you to all

I wonder, because I was born, to make people confuse the psychiatrists first, then my wife my sister my brother who phone hundred times a day, all these people who endure me do not little to endure me. I can't do it anymore, today I'm really sick, and I pray to Jesus that I make me die, so no more boredom to anyone, I can not make it today I'm just sick with this depression dancer that morning I'm sick and the afternoon no. Anyway I thank all these people, who keep me alive who giving me the right medicines and who helps me economically and all those who help me giving me a hope every day for a better day. I want to thank in particular way my wife, who even if she gets angry from the times with me but always she wants me so well. I also thank my brother and sister who do not do little to endure me and always be kind to me. I thank all those who love me, all my relatives both on my side and those from my wife who also want me so well, my father in law my mother-in-law who treated me better than a child even if today there is no longer because she died and to me regret much. Thank you in particular way my mother who put me in the world even though this a dancer brain but it's not her fault is just a disease that is touched on me. I love you so much, mom. Then I thank my father who gave us a road in the work building a factory that keeps us alive today, thank you father for all the love that we give to all of us brothers and sisters, really thank you. In the end I thank my daughter Barbara and Chiara who want me so well and they are my future in this world.

Two beautiful News

Yesterday 24-07-2014 I had two good news, one who wrote to me the secretary of Pope me for the two books that I had shipped to her, the other beautiful news is that the fruit juice of the Arona Melanocarpa has done well to the son of my friend Luciana and my friend Sergio, this girl's disease is to have diabetes since she was a kid at the age of fourteen, and still she is ill.

When I returned to Italy from Poland I brought with me thirty six bottles of Arona, and since or noticed that this fruit juice makes slimming I have given two bottles even to my friend Luciana who is a bit chubby as I am, to see if it slims even she's the way I'm slimming. Had these two bottles there for there was a little disheartened that did well, then looking into the computer all the things that care this plant she decided to take a little bit for morning, too, in addition in the computer found written that this fruit juice is also good for diabetes so she tried to give a little even to her son, and the same day when she went to measure the diabetes she found that she was down enough at once that took this juice of Arona Melanocarpa now I'm curious to know after she took it for a few days as she decreased the diabetes, all this makes me very very happy that this woman can now at least in part to look after diabetes with this fruit. Given that a finger to the reverse brought him diabetes by 150/200 taking insulin, at 100/115 taking even the Arona there is good hopes that this juice of Arona Melanocarpa really works for childhood diabetes associated with insulin also because after having eaten an ice cream the diabetes only climbed to 127 without taking insulin but supported by the

Arona who only takes the morning a finger to the bottom in a glass, filling then water. I hope it with all the heart that works for you that might stand better than for all the children who have this disease.

We useless beings

I am a useless being to the money and profit society, I am a useless being because I do not work and are just a cost to the company that only thinks about the money earned and no to the people who live on this planet, they are like the african countries where the white man looks more to a depredal and a human sense of aid for the development and well-being of the resident populations. I am like a black man seen badly by healthy people who go to work every day and think only to earn as much money as possible, they are just a mental handicapped and nothing more then a useless being to the society of the healthy. Until now I write books that never will read anyone because they are just thoughts of a madman and nothing more, I have a self-esteem to zero because everyone scream me and I break the balls with the phone, but live so better dead. But I do not know what awaits me in life, I love all the people of so continent or state are because I am done so I do not bring grudge to anyone and I feel bad when someone is angry with me I am a bimocking I know but I am done so.

I wish that every state would love all the people not only of their own citizens but also those of other places outside their territory.

Only then will the wars never be made.

The Arona melanocarpa the plant that cares

Today I do not know what to write, but I will try to say something about the Arona This miraculous plant that is still today is not known for all the benefits it can give to the man one thing is certain that a big help can give it to childhood diabetes always with the help of insulin, another certain thing is that it helps to lose weight by removing the acidity of stomach and diminishing appetite this I have experienced on myself, another help gives it to stabilize the blood pressure by reducing the pressure always however with the help of medicines. Then it says that it does well to the heart and the liver in addition says that it does well to the urinary tract, and then enough already seems to me so much however that it does not or the evidence because of these things I do not suffer nor I nor people I know so I can not say for sure.

Nature to know it well always gives us an aid to all our diseases, is that man when he arrives with chainsaws and scrapers and matches It does not look in the face of any plant, and then with the forestry that for large extensions there is only one type of tree takes life to a whole ecosystem provided by more types of trees today missing in our woods. It's going to be until the man comes back the accounts you do not look in the face to any of the ecosystems nor animals plants nothing of anything.

An angel descended from heaven

An angel descended from the heaven just for me... my wife Maria, I write these things because they know my daughters even after dead as well I wanted to my wife Maria, to mummy my dears.

It is just an angel your mother that God has made us know and then marry her I love her so much, we like both the usual things, the flowers for example and what is more beautiful than a flower to this world maybe there is more beautiful two of my girls who in spite of the age always stay in my heart like my two girls.

Remember that daddy to mom has always brought her respect even in the darkest moments of my life when I attempted suicide three times, to mummy my daughters I have always wanted a lot of good because I am so in love.

Remember that when you marry that the first thing in love is to respect each other and this is really the first thing to love and always get along.

I love her so much to my wife I'm just so fond of it and I really like it, because there is no love for interest but it is a true love what I have in my heart.

Dedicated to my wife and daughters

The small dog Lola

My small dog Lola took to the public kennel and waxed so many abandoned dogs all found here in Casentino. Among the many abandoned dogs, my nephew chose her because she was the prettiest and in particular very festive. We had taken to train her to look for porcini mushrooms, it was a little older they had estimated there at the kennel which had over the five years but the age does not count to train a dog as long as one gives her so much affection, we left there on offer of fifty euros we took the dog and we came away. When we arrived at home we had already prepared the fence where to put it, the first days to make her fond of us was tied in the laboratory that so she saw us all the day then in the evening when you stopped working I carried her with me and tried to teach her to sit down giving her good stuff to eat, but taking food from the hand did not take it and did not obey the orders received after two days of trials still to eat by my hand did not take it and by chance my nephew coming to his shoulders he noticed that the dog had not noticed anything of them made some tests to see if it felt we noticed that the dog was deaf. After a few days in the enclosure I decided to take her to my house. With his big heart in the house he bought us all and everyone we fly a lot of good so much is that we went several times in Poland to find my father in law and always brought with us even when he took the airplane.

Teach them to look for mushrooms I did not succeed but I want it too much but so good.

Work four hours and just

I'm repeating this theme, but I'm very much at heart. But because the man has to work eight hours of work to span the family and instead it is not enough four and so give work to all the unemployed who are there today in Italy and in the world, thus giving food to all to the other destination of world population. Also because working around the world eight hours the planet Earth would not make it to hold such production and there would be total destruction of the whole planet to regain itself gives the forests to the seas to all that man can consume, just look here from us in Italy all it is subdued to the service of the man to regain from the forests put all in forestry to arable land that without chemical fertilizer no longer produce anything and to the seas exploited to the maximum until it has served the law to establish when to fish and where to fish and what to fish. If you do not stop a little to reflect on what life is and how enjoy the man will become more and more like a machine that once course is repaired with prostheses of all kinds to make it restart to work the eight hours sacred and untouchable because according to the human mind are indispensable to live you and your family. I think otherwise that a person can live he and his family while working four hours and just because with the technology that exists today the man can grant the luxury of working only the four hours from me repeatedly announced with the usual salary, and the remaining four hours free let them work to another person or who is in the layoff or unemployed. And the four free hours enjoy more life than we have only one and it is right and sacrosanct to enjoy as much as possible.

How to solve this puzzle I do not know, but I am sure that to solve the world crisis that exists today you have to work all and for me the solution can be this "work less but work all and usual salary" if not the crisis does not solve this is my opinion.

We think for a moment to be free

When you arrive at a certain age you realize that it is not worth it to spend all your life inside a factory or in an office or shop that is, all day to work to do that, maybe more houses or sheds than they are, with so many anger because sometimes people don't I pay for the job done, not worth it at all.

We think for a moment if there was no work and being able to do what more do you like how they do in the third world where there are no wars often caused by the white man just to sell more weapons and ammunition, in short we think for a moment to be free to live in the third world where there are no obligations to work to pay taxes but be free, free free, what will we do without the obligation of money and nothing.

I was in Madagascar and I saw these people free from every constraint, it was enough they threw themselves into the sea to procure food and enough they had a little land to breed zebu this African cow that together with chickens provided them the meat to eat. If I had stayed there maybe I would have already died with the disease that I find myself or maybe I would not even go crazy who knows how I would be, bo I do not know what would happen to me. is indeed the third world with the poorest people in the cities that go to rummage in the filthy dumpsters to search for food or who knows what they are looking for. Misery is ugly even if you're free to do what you want to do.

Jesus help me that today I can not live

Jesus please helps me to move forward in life that I cannot do more, with this mental illness that tortures my life. I know I'm a busting balls that call your help a hundred times a day, but without your help, I can't go on in life you give me the hope to get to stay a little better even with the help of medicines. I apologize to Jesus for a bit ugly language, but today it is not life.

I feel you in my sick mind that you always give me good advice, to love everyone, also who detest me, I thank Jesus for the help you give me every day to go on.

Please Jesus help me today is a black day for my mind, the desire to die does not leave me a minute free, I'm really bad help me.

Jesus I love you so much I have read twice the gospel and hope everyone to live a little better to all the sick just ask for your help. Forgive me Jesus for all the sins made in my life especially for the sins made against my planet Earth that I believe are the most serious, I have given death to so many birds that were free in the sky and I shot them and killed them without needing to eat, I regret so much, help me Jesus to forgive me from my planet.

If you are looking for something

If you seek glory they are the most humble of all and the glory will come.

If you're looking for wealth, look at your family and give it a caress.

If you try to command everyone, listen to your heart and everyone's voice.

If you seek the immortality of life they are the most good of all in life.

If you try to make war, think about your dead relatives first and then reflect.

If you seek peace before you apologize for the sins made against everyone you are capable.

If you're looking for health first pray to God to give it to you.

If you are looking for life before you love everyone's life as long as you are alive.

If you seek love open your heart to all and you will see that the love you seek and closer than you think.

If you seek the love of everyone first loves everyone.

If you are looking for the respect of your first door person than everyone then you will have the glory.

If you seek peace in your heart before you love your relatives and then people.

If you seek humility you will be the best of all and close to holiness.

If you're looking for a wife, open your heart to all women.

If you seek holiness before they are the humblest and then will talk about it.

If you try to love the immensity before the land that is your home and then you will see.

If you're looking for something you miss in life before you do family and then love life.

If you're looking for something in your heart, first open it to love.

Two thoughts in one

If you are a mentally ill you lose the esteem of many people, but it is even worse when you lose the esteem of the people you love the most their family their own daughters I am so sad when they respond badly just because I am a dead weight for my family because you can no longer work as they do all. Life unfortunately is so besides being sick for the disease you have to endure this too, fortunately my wife wants me so well that she endures me for my illness, but the estimation of my two daughters I lost it all goes well when they are older with age maybe they will understand that even if I am not a good father, however I want them so well. I write these things because it gets so bad however I shoot ahead until I can.

We change speech in my opinion this world crisis that there is today will not be resolved until we give a job even to the poorest people on the planet and a salary equal to ours, for that I have said so many times, work less hours but work all just so there will be the recovery of the world economy, and no longer exploit the poorest giving him a miserable salary just because to us richer countries back comfortable pay less these people to have low cost products. However it does not touch me to solve these problems, there are so many people who have studied so much that it is up to them to solve these problems, however I think so.

I have to write something

I have to write something, but I don't want to. All these wars that we are around the world feel the desire to live and I like a mockery I'm hurt to know that there is so much hatred among people who shoot against for so many reasons but they are all wrong because they do not kill never a person.

The wars that have always been among men teach us in school as if it were a normal thing that man must do the wars teach him the books of history and whoever wins is seen as a hero a valiant warrior. And the dead people that you don't count are just losers and you don't they mention in the history books how many lives are dead that doesn't count the important is to win the war if you want to be a hero. How much blood has been squandered in the millennia of man's history too much not to understand that we must say enough to the wars, and start a new policy that those who do even to scramble among men is wrong to do so and to school instead of exalting the wars won , teach more than things love among people, one should abolish the books of human history and create books on what is love, love among peoples even if they speak two different languages this is the true story to teach and exalt the good among people and not the evil if you want a society of non-warriors but men who respect each other.

Life is beautiful

Life is beautiful and must be lived in a free way, I'll tell you that I attempted suicide three times and if even if sometimes we feel a bit ' down in the mood you always have to hope that you pass and then come back on to feel good, it tells you one that has the major depression and it takes me so much patience when I'm sick and look for the hope that after everything passes and you return to stay a little better. I especially recommend to you young people that when life goes down in the mood do not seek refuge in alcohol or even worse in drugs I recommend before all this passed by a psychologist or a psychiatrist, there are many medicines to relieve this suffering that you have inside, you never throw your life into a coffin but seek comfort from competent people who are psychologists or psychiatrists will advise you as best as possible for yourselves. Do not think to solve these things alone you will never do it, even I before getting sick I drank a lot of wine I had taken the vice that had my father, I drank not to think of all the problems that wax in my psyche, then I went away from my head and or had the acute psychosis an indescribable thing the suffering that I have passed, so I recommend if life is not good before throwing it away in a dumpster of the filthy past first by people who will advise you as best as possible.

Today I'm just glad

Today I am happy because next week I should give away giving the last giant sequoias remaining of the hundred sequoias that I have borne all gifts are just glad to have made birth are plants endangered and have given a hand to nature so I fill the heart with joy. Hopefully they'll dry a few because hindsight regret me a lot, life is so when you do of the good without interest the heart fills with joy, one thing that I advise you to do is not said that the aid given is to nature but it is better even more if the aid given to both the people who are sick.

Life is funny do things without a logical sense as I did with these sequoias that I made to make here in Casentino the largest Sequoia park in Europe and see that people take you into consideration and do in their chances, the little park of giant Sequoia, is beautiful and I'm glad. I found in the house of my sister of the tiny seedlings of Abies nebrodensis is a plant in the critical area of extinction lived in the Madonie in Sicily there were only thirty specimens that were saved from the chainsaws of man because they were down for a cliff where man could not go, and I recognized this plant that has my sister and I took these tiny seedlings and I put them in pots are left nineteen seedlings and are beautiful, I'm just glad I will plant them in my land where I want to make my park with plants in the way of extinction.

Refugees

Poor Asian Africans come to Italy with these many barges die in the sea close to the mirage of a better life, flee from the war from the misery convinced to find a better world and do not know instead of being locked up all together for a different time before waiting for a let pass so much sighed, convinced to find work and people willing to accept humanely but it is not always so, often exploited to work in the fields to reap the fruits of the earth for a few euros a day and not everyone finds this work, then they are trouble because especially for women they end up working on the streets as prostitutes and men to peddle drugs. For the most fortunate they find themselves in rejoining with their relatives arrived here earlier that are already included in the work and in society. But for many they find themselves in a hostile world with no pity and this to me regret much because they are always people who have behind misery and wars and delude to find Christian acceptance, as the gospel preaches.

The wars from which these refugees flee are very atrocious and they would have all the right to find reception but it is not always so because today we live in misery also

Italian citizens with the precariousness of work that with the global crisis of the economy that is there the whole future is much more black for the fear of finding ourselves without work, even us Italian citizens. That is why I insist on saying that we share this wealth that is the work in four hours per person, and so we will help both our unemployed and there are so many, and we can also help these refugees, making life better for both our workers and this poor gen you who are the refugees.

All this keeping the usual salary and the usual contributions and taxes, so the state will have double fees paid and will reduce taxes in general. However, this reduction in working hours should not be done by a state only of the European Community because if no goes out of the market it would cost a little too much labour, but it must be done by the whole European

Community and if it were possible from all states industrialized world in hindsight this global crisis we're going through doesn't It will go away because there are no new consumers who could be newcomers to the world of work that have to rebuild a better life.

We will not have unemployed and we will have a better life for all employees, above all we will have a more human life for employees who work in factories with chain work and those who work in construction and all those laborious and stressful jobs, making the man freedom to enjoy the life that we have only one and it is not worth throwing it away all in work enjoying only that month the year of vacation if there is money.

And then to each government it is better to have all the citizens working in their own country than to send the work to the foreign, because so the taxes are paid in their own state, and not to the foreign. So this labor that gets us free from the refugees can be our wealth and for a better life for all working only four hours per person with the same salary. To give an example with the fees paid in more by the new employees you could take away all the taxes to the entrepreneurs making it so more palatable to invest in our countries where for the contractor there are no tips fees, just to give an example. And then for a state it is much easier to collect taxes from the workers than by the entrepreneur who try to evade the taxes because they are too high. If it depended on me to the entrepreneur would not to charge him any fee because he has to be rewarded if he invests in our country and gives work to so many people.

Enough to know the right plant that makes for us

It's evening I've already eaten, but I'm still hungry and then I do eat or not, I drink in stead a little ' of arony and now that it is past twenty minutes already I feel full like an egg. This melanocarpa Arona is really miraculous just berne a bit makes me immediately pass the appetite, what a beautiful thing to lose weight with a fruit so natural without tips medicine and without operations, you because the alternative was putting a balloon in the stomach lose weight several pounds and then do an operation in the stomach to then put a wire at the entrance of the stomach to regulate the entry of the food and then this wire tighten it or loosen it according to my slimming, my fear for the operation was fatal I did not want to operate me and I got lucky to find this juice that makes me lose weight making me feel always full stomach and so eat little, what I miss to me is the walk because I'm lazy and so it's not okay I will provide and start walking so I will lose more quickly.

The Aronia, that to the child of my sick friend of childhood diabetes, always taking insulin brought him diabetes values from 150/200 to normal values 100/115. It is true that nature cures all diseases just know the right plant that is for us.

Explanation of the psychosis that will be in the next thought

What patience it takes with mental illness, the psychotropic drugs help you a little but the mood always goes up and down luckily the doctor Sordi told me that when I'm so bad I can take a quarter of lepones and so I can stay a little better but believe me you are so bad with mental illness yet I'll take the medicine always every day but do not do miracles if one does not fall down in a mental illness can not understand how bad it is. In the next thought I want to repropose the psychosis that I had that is tremendous and it is good that people understand the disease in a psychotic state and know how to take remedy quickly both for their safety and for the safety of the sick himself who does not face the evil for himself that for others. I when I had the acute psychosis I was right out of my head and wrote this moment of the beginning of my illness because I will never forget in my life the pain that I have passed and I am one of the few to which the medicines work even if not perfectly whatever I settle and I can at least even write my thoughts right or wrong that may seem. However the important thing is not to have done harm to any person even if I was freaked out.

Psychosis and Delirium

My madness began in the year 1993 in August when in Borgo alla Collina a small village near my house there were to play the Pooh I was sitting in the kitchen in the armchair and I had next to my brother when I began to repent of my sins , I had taken some fruit in the abandoned fields but I began to regret so much, I felt a thief and I was very distressed until I told my brother and asked him why he never told me that, in that way I was stealing, then I went to bed being a little cheered. The next day we were on vacation and I was sitting under the balcony of my house in a rocking when at some point they arrived some of my relatives who had been there for many years, when I saw my cousin Silvia who

I liked even when I was a child the excitement I went to a thousand and I began to hear God talking in my head, and he gave me advice on how I had to behave to go out with Silvia the woman I was in love with at that moment. With the dopamine a thousand, chemical substance that is in our brain and it is the substance of the soul, the next day I went to find where she lived then I found them all from my grandmother and asked Silvia if he wanted to go for a turn in the car in Prato Magno answered yes and with her also came her sister so we will leave all three more my dog Mina that I always took me back. Arrived in the mountain we took a walk in the meadows, but I was very tired because I hadn't slept all night for the excitement that I had taken, I brought them home and saw you again the next day at my house, Silvia had lost her glasses and so they thought that I took it, but actually they were from my grandmother fallen behind the washing machine.

I the next day I went to find them in Prato Magno but I certainly did not find them, only after about a month my grandmother find them behind the washing machine.

My cousin Silvia after she came to my house to look for glasses no longer I saw her, I phoned her the next few days but my head no longer wax I was making speeches according to my delirium and she was very angry and every time I was sick I tried to call her getting worse this situation just until one day I decided not to call her again.

The delirium since I saw her last time was always worse God spoke to me in my brain and always gave me advice constantly did not let me reason a second and told me how to behave with other people, I was also taken a certain excitement when I was talking to a woman and it seemed to me that every woman fell in love with me I was in a addict delirium. Time passed by and the delirium addict became a homosexual delirium and when I saw a man I thought he wanted to do sex with me, the thing terrified me and so I went out of the shed to pray God that helped me not to fall into temptation the thing it repeats for several days, it was all a go and come from the shed I went out to pray and came back to work, as long as the delirium turned into a mystical delirium, I had to become the best of all to overcome even St. Francis in goodness and God who was in my head grumbled me always and told me that I was bad meanwhile had begun to appear the devil in the head and I had begun to terrorize myself I was afraid of all because I saw in them the devil who spoke to me through their mouth their words they were changed according to my delirium, the thing had become terrifying, I was afraid of everyone I thought that with the medicines they wanted me to give me poison so I did not accept that they wanted me to cure. The struggle between God and the devil in my brain had become tremendous, it was enough also the blowing of the wind I thought it was the devil, God grumbled me even when I stomped the grass because it told me that even the grass was alive a living being that must be respected, for some time in the back I looked no longer in the mirror because it was a sign of vanity looking in the mirror. The brain was thinking between God and the devil every rustling every breath that would seam the blowing of the serpent made me think that there was the devil. When I saw the teeth of the people I was scared as if they wanted me to eat or bite and gave me a feeling like it was the devil to show me and he wanted to eat me. I once saw my sister's tongue and one of our clients banging fast as they do snakes, and I thought there was the devil inside them. I slept a few hours three a night and the snoring with my mother's breath terrified me all night because my mother thought she was the head of the devils. Once God told me that I was a devil too, and as such I had to crawl on the ground like a serpent, and so I threw myself to the ground and Imoved as they do the snakes, this because I had dismissed my small dog from Roberto my nephew because in my delirium all the animals were angels of God and with their eyes God looked at us men as we behaved in our planet Earth and so and having removed it from him I had made a big sin because I had alienated an angel from a child. Everything that was happening to me gave me the certainty to live in the earthly paradise with the devil who tortured my life, and God who always grumbled me and told me what I had to do or behave, of course being in Paradise the interview came with the thought where you could talk to everyone but you could not command to anyone and so I was talking with my dog thought, but I couldn't command anything, from the times when I spoke with thought to my family God told me to be silent even with the thought because the devil listens to you, and in the evening when it was darkness God sent me flash of light to warn me that the devil was listening to me my thought so I had to shut up even with the thought, in short I was closed in a deep silence because so much I spoke with all alone with thought and enough. Terror was so much you realize how to see The Exorcist I just got a candle inside.

Remote twenty years I remind the psychic pain that I tried and I will not go away for my whole life what I spent in those three months when I was ill. I do not wish anyone to have a psychosis because it is very bad and the medicine is not that they work very well.

The P.I.L. It is the most important thing.

I regret for this planet Earth does not bring him respect anyone except the men of the forest who surely love the earth and defend it risking life when there are fires often set by the man. This planet that is a marvel at the diversity of plants and animals that are there, today is in danger due to man, the increase of carbon dioxide that modifies the seasons with the greenhouse effect that does not hint to diminish and the man who cuts more and more plants without realizing that already the underwater trees and algae do not make it anymore to absorb all the carbon dioxide produced by the man. It is a suicide that man is trying to make, a planetary suicide because no nation does anything serious to avoid this danger of the air with the carbon dioxide that is increasing and no diminishing. Everyone thinks only of power and does not care about the environment that is in danger, all countries think only about their own economy of P.I.L. That I didn't even understand what it takes instead of thinking about serious things that this planet is destroying and the blame is on the man who is thinking of producing more, for do that then I do not know, instead does not think that it is destroying his house this planet Earth.

A thought so by chance

This morning I don't feel so good, now I took a quarter of lepones by a hundred milligrams that I usually take all the tablet in the evening I do not know this disease destroys me slowly the psyche and makes me want to die, hopefully it does not happen more to take handfuls of tablets as I have done three times, with relative gastric lavande, it is not so good to get a big enough tube from the nose that goes into the stomach to suck all that ingested, it is not for nothing well. Anyway we do not think anymore feel right now that is working the lepones and I'm a little better it takes so much patience believe me with the diseases mental from the times I can't make it anymore then just a quarter of a tablet to retire a little bit on that balls excuse the word used. Who has mental illnesses they are really bad and often people do not understand us and sometimes they are afraid of us and do not want us as friends, I know it is ugly but it is just so often even their relatives do not understand us and we end up being abandoned to our destiny, it is because for normal people we are only a weight in the family, this I regret to say, but we are just a burden for the whole society that does not appreciate us for what we are.

The work

Writing thoughts is not so easy you have to try not to repeat if the book is ugly if you repeat it, however I try to do what I can to not repeat myself. However I enjoy writing because I have no brake points that oblige me to make quick to write a book or other obligations are free to write what I want and I think.

However we change speech, and ugly this global economic crisis, as long as the man will not understand that it is necessary to work less but working all the world economy will never recover because the money of the salaries are given to the few who work and the other nothing must arrange how they can and so exists the work in black. All this is how many people can work more people work more money there are around and the more it gets consumed and the economy so resumes, little money around the economy stops. Everything is up to the governments to choose how many hours must work a worker, the less hours works the more work there will be for another person, the more hours working memo work there will be for other people and so less people consuming and less turns the economy. It is simple to understand it but it is just so that the economy works less people who consume less work there will be for everyone. For the planet Earth is better when people consume less because so there will be more to consume for other living beings and less woods will be sawn to satisfy consumerism, on the other hand more people work less hungry there is around, and the economy resumes for every country that adopts this system less hours of work for each person more people can work. And for today I do not write anymore.

Jesus thank you

Why Jesus took my mind and you modeled it as a selfish miser that I was at one who now loves all people, and my heart rejoices when I do well to someone.

I do not know but I have to thank you Jesus because so I built a family

with the great help of my wife who
helped me in the darkest moments of
my life when or attempted the suicide
three times, and a thank you to the
psychiatrists I've had in these years of
sickness and a thank you also to the
nurses who put us all the heart to give
assistance to all the sick. Thank you
Jesus for all the love you have given me
to love all the living beings of the
planet and especially the love I have for
the plants that I think are the weakest
living beings of our planet, and I have
helped in my little to reproduce them
especially the weakest and in way of
extinction.

O Jesus never abandon my mind
that sometimes I hear you speak, I
know are auditory hallucinations but I
am so pleased to hear you inside me
and talk to me that you always give me
good advice, never abandon me please
Jesus. In these years of sickness you

have changed my life Jesus for the better and I am grateful to you Jesus and I thank you with all my heart.

To enjoy one's life

Life should be enjoyed and not thrown away all in an office or inside a shed because this does not make sense. Many times I think how they are those people who live in the city, with the frantic work returning home that to look for a parking it takes a mountain of time, all that is crazy, or as I did in my life, closed inside a shed for thirty five years, to enjoy that sighed Saturday and Sunday to relax a little, where we even went mad because I could not stand there in the closed for all those hours. What madness all this end up working to do that, an extra house or an extra ground is just madness, give up enjoying life stay outdoors to do walks, know the environment in which you live to learn to recognize the trees, the birds in the sky their tweets fish mushrooms in short all the environment in which you live that for those of city is Arab language, I regret so much that I have spent my whole life inside a shed, I know that to span you have to work but it is enough even less hours of work to live without many ambitions and then I recommend everyone to make and the work you like most without looking at how much you gain if more or less and then have more free time to enjoy this wonderful world.

We are not robots

In the industrialized world it is demanded that the employees of any public body or private company are the machines that once taught what they have to do to repeat it to infinity, but it is not so that the man must be calculated as a robot.

The human brain cannot work endlessly closed inside an office or shed or trades even outdoors we are not machines and we need merriment to get away from the daily routine because hindsight the brain goes on tilt and we end up going crazy or to fall into depression, remember we are not machines and we have to make it clear to those who command us especially the state and the industrialists who calculate people as a workforce and not as people who need their daily leisure if the man is not considered as a human person, you will have a sick society especially of depression as it is already happening.

I admire a dear friend of mine that before I went crazy as I did, he left his beautiful job and he put himself to do

what he likes to work outdoors do what
happens enough to him to live he asks
to make money just for live and should
be so for everyone.

A stroll in Camaldoli

Yesterday August 26 Two
thousand and fourteen I brought to the
hermitage of Camaldoli four giant
Sequoias four Gincobiloba and five
Palms Trachicarpo Fortunei when I
arrived at the hermitage I asked if these
plants would be interested yes or not, a
very kind girl went to ask the monk
that he likes the plants if I could
download them yes or not, the monk
answered yes, this girl I repeat very
kind, has climbed with us in the car to
indicate the road where we had to go to
unload these plants when we arrived to
download the girl asked if I could give
her a palm, when I gave it in the hands
the eyes of the girl begun bright from

the joy. These are the things that fill me with the heart of joy and repay me of all the fatigue to cultivate these plants.

It is so beautiful to give the plants to those who are interested in planting it fills me the heart of joy every time I gift, I am crazy but it is so I enjoy it at that moment that the gift, I will be little stupid but it is so I am happy at that moment. It is so good to know that you do something good for both plants vulnerable to extinction and for the people you offer to plant these plants.

Major depression

The depression that I have is the major depression that when you get the only thought you have is to kill you the desire that you have to die does not leave you escape to other thoughts, you would like to put yourself in a madhouse as a escape to the pain you have as if that of you in a madhouse can be a place to retreat for relief to your psychic pains because you do not make it any more to do anything, all you are doing it costs you a huge sacrifice you don't make it to make even the simplest things because the mood is too down, and then that desire to die that you have does not let you free the thought ever, that's how I attempted suicide three times because I did not do it anymore, the work I had tortured me the conscience because I was in bed and the others worked for me too and that did not seem right and so three times I took handfuls of medicine I wanted to die for not being more weight to anyone. Luckily I have a very good wife who always brought me the emergency room where I have done three times the gastric lavender where you are inserted a tube from the nose and it ends in the stomach and after with a big syringe they extract everything you ingested, I tell you I'm not a pleasant thing. However I wanted to add that the major depression is a bad beast that you can not tame even with medicines because they take effect after fifteen or thirty days, and in that lapse of time you're hurt like a dog clubbed.

Enjoying life

Because in life you have to make all the accounts with money and no longer enjoy your life working less time and devote more time to hobbies that we like the most, I do not understand why, and why those who are at the government will compute us off that miserable salary that suffices us barely to live family if you do not work both in the family if no money is never enough, it is a bad thing as it is now, instead of amusing the man is forced to stay to work all day, it's not right like that. But we hope that those who rule us in the state begin to calculate the wellbeing of a person, how much free time has a person and that we can enjoy more life as possible since we have only one, and it is not better to spend it all the time to work. But life passes it seems slow every day but you find yourself at fifty years in a blink of an eye and it does not seem right that the pension you give it to sixty years when you can not do anything more because you are finished as a person and especially if you have done a job heavy or all day standing.

I recommend to the next generations to struggle to work minus hours and to have retirement at fifty years to have time to enjoy a little more life, in any way either.

We are not the same as the others

We are so different from other, normal people, yes I know we're the crazy people with the altered soul people who if they don't take medicine they get to hear God and the devil speak in their minds, I know they are called auditory hallucinations that only hears our sick mind talking and no other, in addition to this we have visual and olfactory hallucinations and other types of hallucinations that however I did not have and so I do not know about.

I know many people are afraid because many of us do not care and so have a bizarre behavior prone to their delirium and hallucinations.

Life for us is very difficult especially if you get even the depressive

I call it the black beast of mind to always the desire to die until it does the effect of the medicine, then the psychic pain fades but does not pass altogether.

Today the newspapers are full of bad news that make the mentally ill above all of the suffering of depression who also kill their relatives, or schizophrenics who lose control of their gestures if not cured and can do absurd things that they always end up on the front page of the newspapers because the crazy guy who kills always makes headlines and attracts readers. However, we are not all so, there is a majority of mentally ill who care and are well enough and do not give boredom to anyone.

Explanations of some thoughts present in the book

In this book I rewrote three topics also dealt with in the two books that I wrote before and I am: ecology the acute psychosis that I had myself and the major depression that I have always had I do not that the three suicide attempts that I did.

I voluntarily wanted to repeat them to help those who have a mentally ill in the house. I hope who reads will find how painful the mental illness is for the sick and remedy immediately to go to a psychiatrist to be able to give the medicine as soon as possible and be able to take remedy for one's person because even if I have not done harm to anyone when we are in a situation psychotic no longer reason with the head but we are subject to his delirium and is unpredictable behavior of the sick who can do harm to himself or other people.

We hope that these writings will really help you to understand a little better what a psychic illness is and help you to understand the situation of the sick that is the most important thing.

Thank you for having read this book with many good wishes of your health *Antonio Piantini.*

Reviews

By Mom

Bravo,

You know how to express yourself very well it is clear in your view that it is very wise.

Mirella

Romano

I'm reading your last book and I can confirm what Francesco had written, with a small addition:

Your thoughts are beautiful, they manage to condense what would serve for a better world where everyone should want to be well and from this would descend a new social justice, the common good and the joy of living

In this wonderful Earth, instead of destroying
it for human selfishness.

As you know I'm not going through a
good time for my health and this makes me
realize how important the thoughts you write
and how stupid the behavior of most of
mankind is.

An embrace

Romano

Doctor Luigi (psychiatrist)

Once again, Antonio's writings let the
emotional magma flow out of which his spirit
is rich.

The notes in the form of poetry are
certainly more touching than prose.

Amazement and anger arouse the
moments of extreme devaluation that nothing
has to do with his noble soul.

Dr. Luigi

Giulia

It looks like a book of Dreams and Utopias...... but what you say deeply touches the hearts of many and can push them to change and to put a seed for a better world.

It is true that sometimes you "repeat", but it is because those thoughts and hopes are so much alive and deep in you.

Your redwoods, nature, animals, those who suffer those who love are in your thought, in your heart, in your day, in your waking nights.

You are a sensible man who can listen to the forest that speaks, see the little common things, as an immense gift.

You feel God near you perceive his help, his strength his love for you!

I can think of the words that God said to Isaiah when he was lost in courage (Isaiah 41.10). "Do not be afraid, for I am with thee;" Do not look around, for I am your God: For sure I strengthen you for sure I will help you and support you firmly with my right of righteousness. "

Feel pain even for the planet Earth that we are destroying...... but do not fear...... God makes us a promise that will make you happy.

In revelation God says, "I will stop the hand of those who destroy the Earth".

As you see yours are not dreams and utopias, but "healthy" thoughts of those who love life and the world.

Maybe not everyone will like your thoughts, as not everyone will like mine (we are seven billion!!!) But you do well to write them and express yourself and so you will help yourself and who will want to listen to you.

I think of your wife that you love and your girls who are your joy... don't think you're a burden or a nerd... it's your disease that makes you feel like that, your poor self-esteem, your believing you don't do and say what you should!!!

But you are Antonio, unique and unrepeatable with beautiful things and less beautiful things within you, but still the son of God and our brother.

I am sure that your message will remain in the heart and in the memory of many, especially in those you love.

And one day looking at a sequoia or a flower, or a forest...... Your daughter will feel the love you left down here and that your illness failed to choke.

Giulia

Joke:

164

A mentally ill is near the gate of the psychiatric clinic where he is hospitalized.

A passer stops nearby and the sick man says, "We're in here about forty... and from the other side how many are you?"

Dr. Paolo

I wonder and say...

Even in this book, Antonio makes us relive his mental illness, but the thoughts he writes are "Pearls of wisdom", the themes that I face are more than ever present, as we see from the chronicles of these times; and the things you say are not obvious, because there is always need to have them in the mind and heart, if we want to live with dignity.

Dr. Paolo